Original title:
Planetary Puns

Copyright © 2025 Creative Arts Management OÜ
All rights reserved.

Author: Adrian Caldwell
ISBN HARDBACK: 978-1-80567-874-8
ISBN PAPERBACK: 978-1-80567-995-0

Cosmic Caricatures

In the Milky Way, cows float by,
Saying 'Moo-nlight' as they fly.
Stars wear hats, so jaunty and round,
Giggling gently, their joy unbound.

Saturn spins in rings of fun,
Joking with Jupiter, the big ol' sun.
Mars brings snacks to the cosmic dance,
While Venus sways like it's in a trance.

Quasars pulse in a playful tune,
Shooting beams beneath the moon.
Neptune laughs, his winds a-whirl,
Dancing with asteroids, giving a twirl.

Galaxies entwine in winks and smiles,
Light-years dashed in giggly miles.
The universe, a canvas bright,
Painting laughter in the night.

Witty Worlds

In a realm where stars blink,
Planets dance with a wink.
Jupiter's got jokes galore,
While Saturn spins to the floor.

Venus whispers on a breeze,
With humor that aims to please.
Mars cracks up with its red face,
As comets race in outer space.

Celestial Comedy Club

The Moon stood up for a set,
Told a tale we'll never forget.
With meteors as the crowd,
Every punchline drew applause loud.

Asteroids tossed laughs like confetti,
While black holes kept things all steady.
Stars twinkled their eyes in delight,
As laughter echoed through the night.

Cosmic Comic Relief

Uranus chuckled, what a treat,
Said, "I'm gassy, can't be beat!"
Neptune rolled on the cosmic floor,
Shouting, "That's what I'm talking for!"

With giggles heard from afar,
Even Pluto joined in the spar.
Space is big, but jokes are bigger,
In this vast void, we laugh quicker.

Laughter Across Lightyears

With a quip that lights the way,
Lightyears shrink when jokes hold sway.
Zipping 'round at warp speed fun,
Galaxies laugh; what a run!

Puns are like shooting stars,
Falling gently from afar.
Traveling in humor's embrace,
Together we create our space.

Saturn's Rings of Laughter

In a twist of cosmic fate,
Those rings shine bright, truly great!
They dance around planet's waist,
A celestial garment, nothing goes to waste.

Jupiter's jealous, feeling that sting,
But hey, who can resist a bling-bling?
While Mars tries to keep up the chase,
Saturn just laughs, saying, "This is my space!"

Galactic Giggles

Stars tickle comets as they zoom by,
Orion laughs, his arrows awry.
The Milky Way jokes about its cream,
While black holes wonder, "What's their theme?"

Asteroids chuckle, a rocky bunch,
While planets form a very funny hunch.
Neptune's blue, with jokes that they spun,
In the cosmic theater, everyone has fun!

Moonlight Mirth

The moon winks down, a shining prank,
Its craters hide laughter in every flank.
When the sun shines bright, it giggles and glows,
A game of hide and seek, the laughter flows.

Stars conspire with every twinkling light,
Sharing secrets that tickle the night.
While astronauts float in zero-gravity,
They're busting moves—a dance of hilarity!

Spacewalk Smiles

Floating high in the cosmic air,
With a helmet full of puns, who wouldn't dare?
The echoes of laughter bounce off the walls,
As humor ascends beyond Earth's calls.

Cosmic chums with their helmets tight,
Swap jokes like stars soaring with delight.
In this vast expanse, the humor's divine,
Every step taken is a punchline's shine!

The Humorous Universe

In a galaxy far, far away,
Stars twinkle like they've lost their way.
The moon's cheese is aging quite well,
While comets with tails do a slapstick spell.

Asteroids roll like they're in a race,
While meteors giggle with a silly face.
The sun's got jokes, a fiery roast,
As planets circle, they laugh the most.

A black hole takes in all the fun,
Sucking in laughter 'til the day is done.
The rings of Saturn hold a cosmic fair,
Where aliens dance without a care.

So watch for signs in the cosmic light,
As humor shines brighter than stars at night.
In the vastness, joy does accrue,
In the universe where laughter is true.

Galactic Grins

Out in the cosmos where fun is grand,
Stars tickle each other with a twinkly hand.
Pluto joked, "I'm still in the game!",
While planets around him gave him fame.

Venus blushes, a clumsy star,
Tumbling through space like a cosmic car.
Mars chuckles, "My dust is quite thick,"
As rovers gather dust, a humor trick.

Neptune sings high in a watery tune,
While Saturn spins tales on a silver spoon.
Jupiter's storms burst forth in a spree,
With giggles echoing through the galaxy.

In every orbit where laughter spins,
The cosmic stage is set for grins.
So join the jest in a stellar show,
With galactic humor, let your joy flow.

Nonsense in the Nebula

In the nebula, colors collide,
Planets whisper secrets with pride.
Stars wear hats, and moons wear shoes,
While comets fly by with silly cues.

Aliens trade their best dad jokes,
Beneath the starlight, everyone pokes.
Quasars laugh in a light-speed chase,
As black holes grin with an endless embrace.

The Milky Way's a chocolate swirl,
A galaxy where giggles unfurl.
While supernovas pop like champagne,
Creating chaos, yet so much gain.

So dance in the dust, let silliness spread,
In the cosmos' embrace, don't be misled.
For nonsense reigns where starlight sways,
In the nebula of vast, endless play.

Jovial Journeys

On a rocket ship bound for delight,
Astrogators share jokes that ignite.
With every lightyear, laughter does grow,
As space-time tickles, waves of joy flow.

Mercury zips with a playful wink,
While Venus serves tea, don't you think?
Earth spins 'round in a joyous whirl,
As smiles spiral in a galactic twirl.

Mars paints murals in dusty reds,
While Jupiter juggles with humorous threads.
Saturn's rings sparkle with glittering glee,
In jovial journeys across the vast sea.

So buckle up tight, the laughter won't cease,
In the cosmos, find joy, a moment of peace.
For every adventure in the stellar spree,
Is a chance for fun in our cosmic marquee.

Nebula Nonsense

In a cloud of gas with stars that twirl,
The cosmic kittens play and swirl.
Their purrs are light years far away,
Tickling comets in a playful way.

Jazz hands made of stardust glow,
While meteors dance like a Broadway show.
Each twinkle is a chuckle bright,
In the vast dark where they ignite.

Asteroid Antics

Asteroids tumble, giggle, and glide,
Chasing each other in a wild ride.
One trips over a moonbeam's slip,
Says, "I'm just here for the comet's trip!"

With craters full of candy and glee,
They throw space confetti, oh look and see!
Catch a shooting star, it's not a shame,
Being silly in the cosmic game.

Venusian Vau

On Venus's stage, the clouds s
With vapors dancing in a lilac h,
A sly old star plays the guitar,
While planets laugh, saying, "What a s

Giggling gas giants join in the fun,
Juggling moons, oh what a run!
The audience roars, with a burst of light,
As Venus twirls, she takes flight!

Venusian Vaudeville

On Venus's stage, the clouds sing high,
With vapors dancing in a lilac sky.
A sly old star plays the guitar,
While planets laugh, saying, "What a star!"

Giggling gas giants join in the fun,
Juggling moons, oh what a run!
The audience roars, with a burst of light,
As Venus twirls, she takes flight!

Quasar Quirks

A quasar walked into a bar,
Ordered a drink, said, 'I'm a star!'
But the bartender just frowned,
'Still on your way down?'

He chuckled and said, 'That's quite bright!'
'But can you outshine a black hole's might?'
The quasar replied with a grin,
'Only when I've had too much gin!'

The patrons just laughed at the sight,
A quasar causing such a delight!
With light years to travel, it danced,
While others in awe, simply pranced.

So remember, when feeling afar,
You can always reach for a quasar!
Just don't take their jokes too serious,
Or you'll find them rather mysterious!

Stellar Spoofs

A comet zoomed by, full of flair,
Said, 'I'm making a fashion statement up there!'
With a tail that's quite grand,
It's the trendiest in the land!

A dwarf planet chimed in, 'Oh, please!'
'You don't even fit in any galactic lees!'
But the comet just twirled,
'In this universe, I've whirled!'

Saturn wore rings, looking proud,
Said, 'I'm the star of the crowd!'
Jupiter laughed, with a chuckle so wide,
'Let's not forget I have my own pride!'

So in a galaxy that's light and bright,
Everyone's joking, feeling just right.
For the cosmic humor, we must applaud,
In this vast space with laughter, we trod!

Celestial Punslinger

There once was a sun with a pun,
Proclaimed, 'I'm the hottest one!'
But Venus just smirked,
'In a rush, you might get jerked!'

The moons and stars gathered 'round,
To see who could make the best sound.
But Neptune, always so blue,
Said, 'I've got a riddle for you!'

A meteorite threw a good jest,
Claiming it can put humor to the test.
But the stars all rolled their eyes,
'Your jokes are as stale as old fries!'

With laughter, the cosmos rang clear,
Each celestial made jokes without fear.
In this universe, let's all partake,
For humor's the glue that we make!

Comical Constellations

In the night sky, a funny bear,
Waltzed with bright stars, full of flair.
The north star winked, oh what a sight,
'Two left feet under the moonlight!'

An archer shot quips from his bow,
As the sky above began to glow.
'Oh Orion, your belt's out of tune,
Shooting sarcasm under the moon!'

A lion roared with laughter so loud,
'Can we have dinner, I'm hungry, I'm proud!'
The stars giggled, 'What's your main dish?'
He replied, 'Grilled jokes with a side of swish!'

So if you're feeling lost in the night,
Look for jokes that bring pure delight.
In the vastness, you'll find fun's creation,
In every twinkle, a pun's decoration!

Eclipsed Expressions

When the sun and moon dance, oh what a sight,
Shadows play games in the broad daylight.
The stars giggle softly, they can't help but shine,
As the sky plays tricks, a celestial design.

A lunar laugh echoes, 'Why so dark, dear sun?'
'Just playing hide and seek, let's have some fun!'
The cosmos whispers joy, in its own funny way,
As eclipses remind us, it's a bright sky play.

Funny Faces of Phobos

Phobos grins wide with craters galore,
A cheeky little moon, always wanting more.
Behind Mars he hides, playing peekaboo,
'You think I'm small? Well, I dare you to rue!'

With every rotation, he makes a new face,
A cosmic clown dancing in infinite space.
Oh, the Martians chuckle, on this dusty terrain,
As Phobos pulls pranks, never causing disdain.

Witty Worlds Beyond

In the Milky Way's arms, stars wink and nod,
Planets spin tales, it's quite the fraud!
Venus tells jokes, with a sultry grin,
While Saturn on rings, does a romantic spin.

Each world has a punchline, bright and absurd,
With galaxies laughing at every strange word.
A universe jester, floating by night,
Tickling the orbits, it's sheer delight.

Jupiter's Jestful Journey

Jupiter roars with a thunderous laugh,
'Look at my storms, I've got quite the craft!'
With swirling swirls and a Great Red Spot,
He shows off his chaos, like it or not.

A merry giant, he juggles his moons,
While comets and asteroids join in his tunes.
'Is that all you've got?' he teases the rest,
In this cosmic circus, he's always the best.

Planets in Puns

Mercury's quick, always in a rush,
Venus loves love, but it can't hush.
Earth's got a floor, but she also spins,
With her funky moves, she always wins.

Mars is red, a spicy little guy,
Jupiter's big, up in the sky.
Saturn's rings are a fashionable fight,
While Neptune just swims, with all his might.

Uranus jokes, it's known for its name,
Pluto's still grinning, playing it's game.
Celestial bodies, what a goofy crew,
In the cosmic dance, they're all in the queue.

Float through space with a chuckle and cheer,
The stars have humor, let's all draw near.
Galaxies giggle, oh what a sight,
In this celestial stage, everything's light.

Comedic Constellations

Orion's belt, in a funny twist,
Hercules flexes, can't resist.
Cassiopeia poses, such a bright star,
While Leo roars, but he's not the czar.

Taurus the bull, with horns of pure gold,
Claims he sows seeds, but is often cold.
Gemini twins, they're double the laughs,
In a cosmic game of celestial giraffes.

Scorpio strikes with an infinite sting,
But in laughter, finds joy in everything.
Aquarius pours out some giggles and glee,
While Virgo cleans up, sipping her tea.

Sailing through skies, with a wink and a wink,
These stars are here just to make us think.
The universe laughs, oh what a delight,
In the great cosmic circus, everything's bright.

Orbiting Oddities

When Earth spins round, with a grin so wide,
Mars throws confetti, can't let it slide.
Saturn's rings sparkle, like disco balls,
Dancing in space, where the laughter calls.

Pluto's the odd one, still waves goodbye,
"Not a planet," they say, "but I still fly!"
Neptune giggles, with a splash and a dash,
While comets zoom by in a cheeky flash.

Uranus bobbles, the butt of the joke,
Shooting stars throw parties, oh what a poke.
Jupiter laughs, takes it all with ease,
Creating cute storms, like a cosmic tease.

Orbiting whirlwinds, spinning so queer,
Celestial oddities, let's all give a cheer!
A universe filled with joyous delight,
In the cosmic dance, all stars shine bright.

Jovial Journeys

Travel through space, on a giggle ride,
With aliens laughing, all full of pride.
Rockets take off with a honk and a cheer,
As stars twinkle down, saying, "Welcome here!"

Mars roller coasters, not quite so rough,
But Venus tells tales, a bit too tough.
Saturn swings low, with rings that just shine,
While Jupiter's laughter is simply divine.

Floating through Saturn, what views to behold,
A cosmic ballet, with humor untold.
With Pluto still munching on frosty delights,
In this space adventure, our joy ignites.

Each journey out here, a comic affair,
With laughter that sparkles, hanging in air.
So grab your spacesuit, let's all take a flight,
To the jestful cosmos, where everything's light.

The Comedic Constellation

Stars giggle in the night,
As planets dance in sight.
A comet's tail wags with glee,
'I'm flyin' high, just wait and see!'

Saturn's rings give a twirl,
While Mars tries to flirt a whirl.
Venus jokes with a wink,
'I'm hotter than you think!'

Uranus rolls off a jest,
'I've got no rings, but I'm the best!'
Neptune, with a sigh, replies,
'I'm just here for moonlit skies!'

In the vast and bright expanse,
Celestial bodies love to prance.
Each twinkle holds a silly tale,
In the cosmos, humor will prevail!

Lunar Laughter

The moon thinks it's a great chef,
Making craters like it's deft.
'Turn your light into dessert,
Watch my cheese with stars alert!'

In dark skies, the laughs do bloom,
The sun can't help but join the room.
Stars shout, 'This is quite the show,
Let's joke around, just so you know!'

Tides yank laughs from the sea,
'Hey, moon, you're twinkling for free!'
A lunar giggle fills the night,
Echoing in silver light.

With each phase, a pun is shared,
Full of humor, none are scared.
Lunatics in the skies above,
Inviting all to share the love!

Zany in Zero Gravity

Floating jesters in space, it's a sight,
Drifting by, causing pure delight.
With zero gravity, jokes take flight,
Laughing stars shine with all their might.

Galactic clowns swoop and spin,
They tumble like they're in a win.
'Why don't asteroids ever play?
Because they might just asteroid away!'

In the vacuum, silliness sways,
As aliens laugh in cosmic bays.
Space ships honk with comedic flair,
While echoes of giggles fill the air.

In a world where laws are bent,
Every zany joke is heaven-sent.
Gravitational pull lost to the fun,
In zero gravity, we all are one!

Humor on the Helix

Twisting around in cosmic threads,
Where laughter weaves and humor spreads.
'Why did the galaxy take a trip?
To see the stars and give them a quip!'

On helix paths, the comets zoom,
While black holes fashion their own room.
'Stay away from that event horizon,
It's the ultimate unscheduled risin'!'

Nebulas chuckle in every hue,
Colors sparkle, bringing joy anew.
'Why pick a star? They're all so bright,
But I'm light years away tonight!'

Galaxy-wide, the giggles float,
On stellar winds, they rise and gloat.
In the cosmic spiral, humor's the key,
Join the dance, just you and me!

Comet's Quirky Tales

A comet zooms, it's quite a show,
With tail so bright, it's hard to slow.
It skips past Mars, shouts, "Catch me soon!"
And dances 'round the silvery moon.

It flirts with stars, gives them a wink,
With fiery trails that make you think.
"I've got a speed that's out of sight!"
Chasing shadows in the quiet night.

It tells of friends that are out of reach,
Like sneaky planets that just won't teach.
"Oh, how they like to brag and boast!"
As it whirls past, the brightest ghost.

With its comet's charm, it spins a tale,
Of cosmic pranks that never pale.
In the vastness of space, it stirs up fun,
With a wink and a smile, it's never done.

Saturn's Sarcasm

Saturn spins with rings so grand,
"I'm the best! Please understand!"
A disco ball in cosmic style,
While other planets wear a frown, not a smile.

"Oh, Jupiter, you're big and bold,
But I'm the one with charms untold!"
As asteroids laugh, they twirl and glide,
Catching Saturn's sass as it takes a ride.

"I can't see your moons, they're quiet, right?
Mine are dancing, oh what a sight!"
While rings twinkle in jovial jest,
Each loop and swirl is truly the best.

With sarcasm shining, it spins with glee,
"Let's get together, it's all about me!"
In the cosmic ballet, its humor flows,
As it pirouettes where the stardust glows.

Celestial Circus

Welcome, one and all, to the grand show,
Where stars juggle planets and comets glow.
With Saturn on tightrope, what a sight!
And Martian lions roaring in delight.

Venus is the ringmaster, taking the lead,
With a wink and a smile, to charm and to plead.
"Ladies and gents, prepare for the thrill!"
As asteroids tumble, the crowd's fit to spill.

Uranus on stilts sways to the beat,
While playful moons twirl on tiny feet.
"Look at me dance! I'm quite a breeze!"
As meteoroids cheer from the cosmic seas.

The sun's a bright spotlight, shining down,
On this celestial circus, the best in town.
With laughter and joy lighting up the night,
The universe giggles, what a delight!

Jupiter's Jests

Jupiter chuckles, the king of the space,
With a giant red spot, it's a goofy place.
"Why did Mars blush? It saw me prance!"
As the gas giant begins to dance.

"I'm the biggest, but jokes are my game,
Will you join me or are you too tame?"
With swirling clouds that tickle the prude,
Jupiter's humor is never rude.

Satellites giggle at each funny quip,
As they orbit around, they flip and dip.
"You say you're fast? Try keeping up!"
As it races past, an interstellar pup!

With jests that ripple through the vast night,
Jupiter spins tales that feel just right.
In the cosmos bright, laughter ignites,
As the jovial giant shares its delights.

A Comet's Quip

A comet whizzes by with flair,
It trails a smile up in the air.
"Don't judge my speed, I like to race,
I'm always late, but just in place!"

Through space it dashes, quick and bright,
With cosmic jokes that feel just right.
"I'm on a roll, can't you tell?
I'm here for laughs, I'm outta shell!"

Around the stars it spins and plays,
Cracking jokes on stellar rays.
"I've got a tail, what's your excuse?
My love for puns is a no-use!"

So hitch a ride, don't miss the fun,
A comet's life is never done.
With laughter echoing in the void,
Some cosmic smiles can't be avoid!

Joking in the Milky Way

In the Milky Way, stars twinkle bright,
They share their jokes in the cold, dark night.
"Why was the planet a bit blue?
It thought it lost its rings—who knew?"

The stars chuckle, light years apart,
Each punchline sung in stellar art.
"What did Jupiter say when it spun?
I'm just a gas king, having fun!"

Galaxies swirl with laughter wide,
Each supernova a cosmic guide.
"Why don't aliens ever get lost?
They follow the stars—they like the cost!"

As comets zoom with witty charm,
Their humor keeps the cosmos warm.
In the Milky Way, joy ignites,
With silly quips that spark delight!

Mars' Mischief

On Mars, the rovers roll with glee,
Hunting for water and a cup of tea.
"Why did Mars apply for a job?
I needed work, or I'd just blob!"

Red dust swirls with laughter high,
While Martian pranks catch yellow eye.
"What do you call a Martian, sly?
A plan-it-of-mars—oh my, oh my!"

As sunsets glow in shades of rust,
The Martians giggle—this is a must.
"Why is Mars such a great host?
It has a crater for the most!"

When rovers tell their tales of joy,
Mars just grins, a playful ploy.
With mischief brewing in the air,
Every laugh is a cosmic dare!

Celestial Snickers

In the cosmos, laughter never ends,
With celestial snickers shared with friends.
"Why don't stars ever get cold?
They wear their blankets of space—so bold!"

Galaxies twirl, with grins so wide,
Each nebula a chuckle, can't hide.
"What did the moon say to the sun?
I'm waxing poetic—oh, this is fun!"

As asteroids tumble, filled with cheer,
Their rocky tales can't disappear.
"Why did Saturn break up with Mars?
Too many rings—they're too bizarre!"

So with each comet flying high,
The universe bursts with laughter nigh.
In celestial realms, joy is shared,
As humor dances, none impaired!

Cosmic Comedy Club

In the Milky Way, laughs abound,
Stars twinkle with a chuckle sound.
Black holes don't take things slow,
They suck in jokes, and off they go.

Jupiter's got its moons in tow,
Their dance is all for the show.
Venus slips on a cosmic rhyme,
Saying, "Let's keep it light during our time!"

Mars cracked a pun, a real knee-slapper,
Claiming all its red is just a capper.
While Saturn's rings spin tales so wide,
They can't keep a straight face, oh what a ride!

Galaxies swirl in a laughter trance,
As comets join in the cosmic dance.
Join the fun, don't sit alone,
In this space club, we call it home.

Laughing with the Light-Year

A light-year's journey, so full of cheer,
Ever so bright, the jokes are near.
Traveling fast at the speed of wit,
Laughter echoes, we just can't quit.

Nebulas swirl in colors so bold,
Telling tales that never grow old.
A quasar's giggle, brilliant and bright,
Makes even black holes beam with delight.

Asteroids crack jokes that bounce and roll,
While shooting stars wish for laughter whole.
A comet's tail, a punchline in flight,
Zooming past with a giggle at night.

With every tick of the cosmic clock,
Our giggles echo, oh what a shock!
The universe smiles, not a frown in sight,
Laughing with stars, everything feels right.

Giggle on the Event Horizon

At the edge where light takes a bend,
Horizon giggles as time does send.
Come dive into darkness, take a spin,
Carry your laughter, let the fun begin.

Gravity pulls on every good joke,
Twisting the truth, a cosmic poke.
Einstein chuckles, he knows the score,
Relativity's just humor's core.

Silly photons take a leap in jest,
Witty waves laughing, feeling blessed.
Hawking smirks as he tosses one more,
"A laugh a day keeps the void from the door!"

So gather 'round as we play and tease,
In the folds of spacetime, ride the cosmic breeze.
Each punchline a trajectory, tickling the night,
At the event horizon, everything feels right.

A Probe into Puns

Our probe set forth with a snicker and jest,
Seeking out humor, oh what a quest!
Voyager whispers to Saturn's rings,
"What's your favorite of all human flings?"

Mars laughs back, in its red, dusty way,
"I tell Earthlings, stop sending those cliché!"
Pluto chimed in, feeling rather bold,
"I may be small, but I'm pure gold!"

As we glide past comets, we hear their song,
A chorus of laughter that's bright and strong.
Jupiter's moons join in with a cheer,
Making the silence disappear.

In this cosmic voyage, we spread the joy,
No matter the distance, puns we'll employ.
Exploring this vastness, remember the fun,
A probe into laughter, we've all just begun.

Orbital Oddities

In a galaxy far, we spin and twirl,
Stars play tag, while comets whirl.
The moon said, "Earth, you've got some weight!"
"Yes, I'm grounded, and it's not too great!"

Saturn's rings are bling in space,
Jupiter laughs, it's a giant race.
Uranus giggles with its tilted style,
"I'm just here for a cosmic smile!"

Venus blushes, always so bright,
Says, "I'm the gem of the night!"
But Mars just chuckles with rusty flair,
"At least I've got the best dust to share!"

Mercury zips, a speedy show,
"Can't catch me in the cosmic flow!"
Each world takes turns in the cosmic jest,
In this grand dance, who's the best?

Celestial Comedy

In the sky where the asteroids roam,
One called Rocky said, "I'm far from home!"
Laughter echoes, a celestial choir,
As meteors fall like a shooting shyer.

Neptune's blues sing a humorous tune,
"I'm just here for a watery swoon!"
While Pluto quips, "I'm not a planet, it's true,
But I'm still small enough for a cosmic review!"

Stars put on jokes, a cosmic ballet,
Galaxies swirl in a playful display.
"Why did the black hole apply for a job?
It wanted to attract, not just mob!"

Each quasar beams with illuminating cheer,
And cosmic dust dances without any fear.
Together they spin, a light-hearted spree,
In the universe's play, forever carefree!

Milky Way Mirth

In the Milky Way, there's a chocolate bar,
Cowboys ride comets, they're never too far.
A starry wink from the wide open sky,
Says, "Life's a treat, let out a sigh!"

The sun cracks jokes, with warming rays,
"Why don't we get weekends? I love sunny days!"
While black holes whisper, with mysteries thick,
"We keep things mysterious, it's our little trick!"

Venus and Earth host a giddy tea,
"Is it steamy enough, or needs more spree?"
Mars tosses peanuts with a playful grin,
"I'm red with laughter; let's all jump in!"

Halley's Comet rushes with glee,
"I'll stop by for tea, count on me!"
Meanwhile, orbiting pals share a laugh,
In this cosmic tale, we're all part of the path!

Nova Nonsense

When a nova bursts, it's quite the show,
Stars blink and giggle, putting on a glow.
"What do you call a bright supernova?"
"A stellar pop, it's a heavenly soap opera!"

Galaxies twirl in a dance so fine,
"Let's mix and mingle over starlight wine!"
One dwarf planet sneezes, and everyone chuckles,
"Bless you, my friend, through the cosmic huddles!"

In the Andromeda, they hold a feast,
With quasars as desserts, the laughter's increased.
A giggle erupts from a twinkling star,
"I'm shining so bright, you can see me from afar!"

As the cosmos spins, with humor and delight,
The universe busts jokes into the night.
In this vast space, no reason to frown,
We're all just jokes in the heavenly town!

Martian Mirth

On Mars, the red dust gives quite the thrill,
Rovers roll by, their wheels seem to chill.
They shout, "Hey, look! We're drilling for jokes!"
"Just mining for laughter, you Earthling folks!"

In the craters, there's laughter, a jovial cheer,
Can aliens dance? We'd love to see here!
With space helmets bouncing to a beat,
They're plotting a show that's surely a feat!

They've spotted some water, oh what a tease,
"A cocktail of comets! Pour us some freeze!"
In games of tag, they float with such grace,
The Martians proclaim, "We're the best in this space!"

So if you're feeling down or blue,
Just think of their giggles, a cosmic view.
With laughter so grand on a Martian day,
You'll grin with the stars, then float away.

Jovian Jest

Around Jupiter, the storms are a show,
"Why did the lightning bolt cross the glow?"
To brighten the darkness, oh what a pun!
"I'm just shocking everyone, oh isn't it fun?"

With moons of all sizes, they're dancing in lore,
"Why did the satellite ask for more?"
"I need some support, I'm feeling so blue!"
Yet spinning and twirling, they twinkle, it's true!

The Great Red Spot is a swirl with a grin,
"Let's have a party; we're livin' to win!"
They mix up some gas, with a splash of delight,
And sing, "We're the reason for planetary light!"

They joke with the comets, the asteroids too,
"Did you hear about Saturn? He's gaining more blue!"
With giggles that echo through space without end,
Jupiter's jovial, the fun never bends.

Saturn's Satire

Oh Saturn, with rings that twirl and dance,
"Why's the ring always late to enhance?"
"Because it's got a lot of sharp turns to take!"
It laughs with a wink, what jokes it can make!

The moons whisper softly, sharing their schemes,
"Can we be the stars in a celestial dream?"
Then chuckle together, tumbling around,
In a waltz of light where no sadness is found!

"What did the planet say to the star?"
"I feel so alone, can you come from afar?"
And the star just replied with a bright, shiny flare,
"Just follow my glow, I'll always be there!"

In the orbits they spin, with humor so bright,
Saturn holds court, in the deep velvet night.
With laughter that echoes across cosmic space,
The universe giggles, what an amusing place!

Comet's Comical Grace

A comet streaks by with a tail of great flair,
"Why don't we hang out? There's fun in the air!"
Faster than whispers, it zips through the skies,
"I'm just chasing dreams; look how bright I can rise!"

With each cosmic stroke, it paints trails of fun,
"I'm the celebrity; can't you tell I'm the one?"
"I dart and I giggle, through galaxies vast,
My sprite-like existence goes by in a blast!"

"Did you hear about gravity? Tried to hold me tight,
But I said, "No thanks, I'm just flying tonight!"
As stars roll their eyes, the universe sways,
And laughs out aloud in a marvelous craze!

So if you see light, in the night's tender lace,
Know it's just me having comical grace.
In my fleeting moments, I bring joy and cheers,
As I whiz through the cosmos, shedding light on your fears!

Solar System Satire

In the Sun's hot rays, we gather near,
While Mercury spins, it can't stand the cheer.
Venus might be lovely, but it's quite a tease,
With clouds of acid, it's not a place to please.

Earth plays the host, we're all invited,
But next to Mars, we feel so slighted.
Jupiter's great, but storms never cease,
While Saturn's rings say, "Hold on for peace!"

Uranus spins sideways, what a strange twist,
While Neptune's deep blue makes the sailors mist.
To travel the stars, what an expense,
But this cosmic circus makes perfect sense!

Interstellar Irony

In space there's no air, we hear them say,
Yet astronauts take their breath away.
Black holes are weird, they swallow it all,
Pluto's a planet, or so we recall.

The Milky Way's thick, but we're slim on news,
What's the scoop on the cosmic blues?
Aliens laugh from their distant star,
At all of our selfies, taken from afar.

Gravitational pull, a weighty affair,
While flying through comets, we lose our hair.
The cosmos is full of whimsical charms,
And the void just giggles with open arms!

Lightyear Laughs

Lightyears away, the stars have a ball,
With twinkling jokes, they beckon us all.
What do you call a star that likes to play?
A real twinkler, shining night and day!

Comets with tails, they dash by so fast,
"Catch me if you can!" is their playful cast.
Asteroids crash, they have no regrets,
While meteors streak, like cosmic marionettes.

Time is a riddle, in lightyears we roam,
Each galaxy whispers, "Make yourself at home!"
NASA's on standby for moments so rare,
As laughter echoes through infinite air!

Cosmic Capers

On Mars, the rovers dance in delight,
While Venus bakes cakes in the heat of the night.
Jupiter's moons have a party so grand,
While Saturn's rings play a band on demand.

The asteroids joke, "We're rock-stars, you see!"
While Uranus grins, "I'm the life of the spree!"
Neptune's deep secrets bubble and brew,
With laughter that echoes, "What's new, what's new?"

In the void of the night, the stars trade their puns,
Making light of our trips and our interstellar runs.
With cosmic capers and villains so sly,
The universe chuckles at us, oh my!

Nebulae Nonsense

In the heart of the stellar spree,
Gas clouds giggle, wild and free.
Stars wink with a sparkling flair,
While galaxies swirl in a cosmic prayer.

A meteor quips with a comet's tail,
Shooting across the night with a tale.
'Why don't astronomers like the moon?'
'Because it's always shining too soon!'

Asteroids bump with cheeky glee,
'You're a little rocky, just like me!'
Saturn spins in rings of jest,
Making fun of who's the best dressed.

So when you gaze up, join the dance,
With all the orbs, take a chance!
For in the cosmos, laughter does dwell,
In nebulae nonsense, we're under a spell.

Astronomical Antics

Why don't we ever tell secrets to stars?
Because they might just burst into cars!
Galaxies giggle, in spirals they twirl,
As supernovae puff out their curls.

Uranus jokes in the outer zone,
'You think you're cool, but I'm all alone!'
Mars grins wide with its rusty red,
'At least I'm no longer a fruit's spread!'

Black holes chuckle at missing socks,
'You'll never see them, we're the paradox!'
Planets parade in a jovial line,
Each one cracking jokes that are simply divine.

So come and join the celestial fun,
Where even the stardust can crack a pun.
In astronomical antics, the lighthearted play,
Reveals the universe's silly display.

Cosmic Jesters

In the vastness, where comets fly,
Cosmic jesters wink and sigh.
'Hey, Sun, you're burning bright,'
'But your jokes are always out of sight!'

The Moon laughs at Earth's messy face,
'You clean up well, but what a race!'
Shooting stars dash with glee and flair,
'Wishing on us? Oh, such a scare!'

Pluto pouts in a distant cold,
'When I was young, I was bold!'
But the others beam with humor's grace,
'You'll always have a special place!'

So as you gaze at the night so grand,
Remember the jokers, hand in hand.
In the realm of cosmic jesters, so bright,
Laughter reigns supreme in the starry light.

Comet's Chuckling Cradle

In a cradle of dust, a comet rolls,
Chasing stardust while cracking bowls.
'Why did the black hole cross the road?'
'To eat a star, lighten its load!'

Jupiter jumps, all fun and wide,
'These storms of mine? It's just my pride!'
With rings of laughter and moons of cheer,
Saturn smiles, 'Come lend an ear!'

Neptune whispers deep blue dreams,
While winking stars burst at the seams.
'You think it's chilly, but what a show!'
'It's the laughter that keeps us aglow!'

So when you're lost in the cosmic race,
Remember the comets and their playful pace.
In the chuckling cradle of the night,
The universe tickles, oh what a sight!

Gravity-Defying Giggles

In a world where weight means little,
The moon jokes with the stars, what a riddle!
Saturn spins with its rings all around,
While comets giggle and dance, unbound.

Mars rolls its eyes at the Earth's blue hue,
Says, 'You're too plain, I'll outshine you!'
Jupiter laughs, with a stormy grin,
'Just wait until I let my winds begin!'

Venus winks at the sun with a glare,
'You think you're hot? Oh, please, beware!'
Mercury zips, all fast on its track,
'Catch me if you can, I won't look back!'

In this cosmic circus where humor flies,
The laughter echoes through the skies.
So let's all join in the galactic cheer,
For the universe knows how to joke, I fear!

Whimsical Wavelengths

In a dance of light, the stars align,
Sending giggles through the cosmic vine.
Neptune hums a tune with a splash,
While Pluto teases—'Call me a has-been, you trash!'

Black holes munch on quips, like snacks,
'What's more fun than light? Oh, I'll take that!'
A nebula bursts into laughter so bright,
Colors swirling in the dark of the night.

Pulsars pulse jokes, in beats they rotate,
'Time is funny when you're never late!'
Asteroids tumble, with humor unshy,
'Let's rock this universe, oh me, oh my!'

As wavelengths blend in a giggly display,
Let's surf the cosmos, come join the fray!
For laughter exists in this vast, starry bay,
In every corner where stardust will play.

Cosmic Chronicles

Once upon a time, in galaxies far,
Aliens chuckled beneath a bright star.
They shared tales of comets with tails that swish,
And planets that wished on a starlit dish.

Uranus snickers at its own bold spin,
'What's so funny? I've got gas from within!'
Venus looks coy with a wink and a sigh,
'Who needs green when you've got a radiant sky?'

Solar flares dance in a fiery jest,
'Let's ignite the night—who's up for a quest?'
Constellations giggle as they twirl in the void,
Painting stories with stardust, never annoyed.

Thus, in the realm where humor takes flight,
Every twinkling star brings a spark of delight.
So gather around for laughter's embrace,
In this cosmic tale, we all find our place.

Stellar Shenanigans

In the midst of the stars, a party takes place,
With meteor showers and cometary grace.
Asteroids roll with a raucous cheer,
Saying, 'Join the fun, there's nothing to fear!'

Lunar landscapes echo with giggly refrains,
As space cows moo in the moonlit plains.
Black holes whirl with a cheeky grin,
'Care to play hide and seek? Just jump in!'

A rogue planet wagged its dusty tail,
'You'll never catch me, I'm off on a trail!'
Galactic shenanigans fill the wide scope,
Where humor and wonder create boundless hope.

So lift your gaze to that infinite sea,
Where laughter is cosmic and wild and free.
To the rhythm of stars, let your worries unbind,
In this whimsical dance of the universe, find!

Astronomical Amusements

Why did the sun get a ticket so bright?
For shining too loud in the neighbor's night.
The moon said, 'I'm just here to reflect,'
While stars whispered secrets they hoped to protect.

Jupiter tried to dance, oh what a sight!
But all of his moons didn't think it felt right.
They spun in delight, twirling around,
While Saturn just laughed with his rings spinning sound.

Mars wore a helmet and claimed he's a knight,
Guarding his craters with all of his might.
Venus, with style, said, 'I'm dressed to impress!'
But Mercury teased, 'That's just pure excess!'

With comets all tailing, they raced through space,
Finding new worlds in a humorous chase.
Galaxies giggled as they twinkled so bright,
In this cosmic dance, oh what a delight!

Milky Way Merriment

A comet passed by with a glorious grin,
Saying, 'Catch me if you can, where to begin?'
The stars in the crowd all gave a loud cheer,
While black holes just laughed—'We'll pull you in here!'

The planets formed lines, a cosmic parade,
Each boasting of quirks, none were afraid.
Earth joked of its selfies from space up above,
While Pluto just sighed, missing all the love.

Neptune wore shades, claiming to be cool,
But Uranus chimed in, 'Don't be a fool!'
Then Venus threw a party, with cupcakes so sweet,
And all of the dwarfs danced on their feet.

The moons held their breath in the stellar fun,
As meteors raced, their wishes begun.
In the Milky Way's arms, laughter's embrace,
In this whimsical world, we find our place.

Laughter in the Cosmos

Black holes are hungry, they'll swallow a star,
And ask for more snacks, as if they're bizarre.
While stars in the sky play hide and seek,
Nebulae giggle, 'We're just too unique!'

The sun wears a hat, claiming it's hot,
While Venus adds, 'We'll give it a shot!'
Mars cooked some rocks, declared it a stew,
While Saturn just laughed, 'It's more of a to-do!'

As comets zoom past, they whistle a tune,
Singing of adventures from June to the Moon.
Galaxies waltz in a spiral delight,
Twinkling together, what a magical night!

It's a universe bursting with joy and with jest,
Where laughter and light make the cosmos the best.
In this infinite play, where the fun never dies,
We're all just stardust under luscious skies!

Uplifting Orbits

In a galaxy bright, where silliness grows,
Mars drew a smile that everyone knows.
With meteors falling, making a show,
They painted the night with a cosmic glow.

Uranus rolled in with an outlandish pride,
Saying, 'I'm just quirky, there's nowhere to hide!'
While Jupiter chuckled, with storms he would boast,
'You're just too funny, you're my favorite host!'

The asteroids lined up, dancing in rows,
Shaking and shimmying, striking cool poses.
And comets all trailed with sparkles in air,
Creating a spectacle, joyful with flair.

In this lighthearted space, we'll always find fun,
With each little orb, laughs have just begun.
So let's raise our voices, oh what a delight,
In these uplifting orbits, we shine through the night!

Cosmic Caprices

In the vastness, stars so bright,
One twinkled, saying, "What a sight!"
The moon chimed in with a cheeky grin,
"I'm just here, looking to win!"

Planets dance in a stellar ball,
Saturn's rings? They seem to enthrall.
But Neptune whispers, "Do I look blue?"
"Only when I'm near you!"

Mars threw dust, a flashy show,
"Don't get too close! I might throw!"
Jupiter laughed, with a thunderous sound,
"I'm just full of gas, keep spinning 'round!"

Asteroids roll in a playful race,
"Watch me zoom, I'm up in space!"
While comets giggle, tails held high,
"We pass by fast, just to say hi!"

Meteoric Merriment

Shooting stars leave trails so rare,
"Catch me if you can, if you dare!"
A comet grinned, with a dazzling wake,
"I'm the fastest treat you'll ever bake!"

In orbit, satellites spin in glee,
"I dance around like it's just me!"
The sun made jokes, with a fiery flare,
"You think I'm hot? Just look at my hair!"

Astrology's quirks, they take to heart,
"I'm a Capricorn, and that's just the start!"
While a Libra joked, "I keep it fair,
Balance is key, so a little flair!"

Space-time giggles, it's quite a stretch,
When black holes tease, "Come and fetch!"
With gravity's pull, they spin and swirl,
"I'm just playing, give it a whirl!"

The Jovian Jokester

Jupiter's storms are wild and loud,
"I'm the king, and I feel so proud!"
With swirling clouds, he cracks a joke,
"I'm so big, not sure I'd choke!"

His moons chime in, a merry crew,
"What's the latest? Tell us, do!"
"Stop orbiting around, do join the fun!"
"We'll prank the sun, till the day is done!"

Io's got volcanoes, a fiery zest,
"I'm just blowing off some steam; no rest!"
Europa smiles, with ice so neat,
"Under my cover, life would be sweet!"

They gather round for a cosmic chat,
"Who's the biggest? Well, imagine that!"
A game of size in the great expanse,
"In this wide universe, let's all dance!"

Cosmic Capers

In the galaxy's twist and swirling spree,
"I'm the star that twinkles for all to see!"
A nebula sighed, full of colorful hues,
"Painting the sky was my kind of muse!"

The Milky Way joked, "I'm quite the blend,
With all my stars, I can't ever end!"
While black holes play peekaboo,
"Come on in! I dare you!"

Stars and planets share a giggle fit,
"Hey, did you hear? We're all a bit lit!"
The cosmos chuckled in unison wide,
"In this great void, we all slide!"

From quasar to quasar, the fun's never done,
"In the infinity of space, we all are one!"
So let's raise a toast with our cosmic cheer,
To humor and joy throughout the year!

Galaxial Gigglefest

In a nebula of laughter's flight,
Stars twinkle with pure delight.
Planets spin in merry jest,
As comets humorously quest.

Mars may boast of iron might,
But Venus steals the cosmic light.
Jupiter's storms, a wild parade,
While Saturn laughs, its rings displayed.

Asteroids tumble in a song,
Singing to the stars all night long.
Black holes with jokes that pull you near,
They suck you in, but don't you fear!

In this giggling galactic spree,
The universe grins, wild and free.
Cosmic chuckles, a stellar show,
Join the fest; we're ready to go!

Moonlit Mischief

Under the glow of the silvery orb,
The stars wink with a cheeky sorb.
Jokes bounce off the lunar beams,
As meteors chase their wild dreams.

Cheeky aliens pop in for fun,
Spreading jokes as they slyly run.
Satellites giggle in orbit so wide,
While the sun grins, all full of pride.

Eclipses hide with a clever tease,
And constellations play in the breeze.
Comets crack up, tails all a-flare,
In this moonlit mischief, no woes to spare!

With each tick of the cosmic clock,
The universe rocks, a jovial shock.
Join the mischief, dance in the light,
Where the moon's laugh echoes through the night!

Universal Humor

From black holes come laughs that are strange,
In the vacuum, scents of humor exchange.
Galaxies spin with a punchline twist,
Creating a cosmos that must not be missed.

Supernovae burst with a comic flare,
As laughter rockets through space's air.
Aliens chuckle with quirks so grand,
In this universal dance, take a stand.

Light-years are crossed in a playful race,
Where every star wears a smiling face.
Planetary jokes made with a wink,
Even asteroids find time to think!

So grab your laughs, let humor reign,
In this cosmos, lose all strain.
Universal chuckles, nothing to fear,
Join the fun; the laughs are near!

Starstruck Smiles

Every twinkle tells a tale so bright,
Stars shining down, a pure delight.
Meteor showers crack a good one,
While Saturn's rings spin twice the fun.

Asteroids roll with a jovial leap,
While galaxies around them softly creep.
A wink from a nova, glittering tricks,
Lunar laughter that always clicks.

Orbits dance in a merry cascade,
With every revolution, new jokes are laid.
Cosmic entities in giggles unite,
As starstruck smiles light up the night!

In this realm, where joy takes flight,
The universe glows in pure delight.
Let's gather under this starry dome,
With laughter and love, we'll find our home!

www.ingramcontent.com/pod-product-compliance
Lightning Source LLC
Chambersburg PA
CBHW071818160426
43209CB00003B/133